CHINCHU GETS A SUPERPOWER! (GIRLS EDITION)

M PATTABIRAMAN

Made with ♥ on the Notion Press Platform
www.notionpress.com

Contents

Acknowledgements

Several people have helped me put this book together. My wife Rama and son Srikanth have helped me fine-tune several aspects of the book. Rama shared her insights on astronomy, which made my life simple in the last chapter. Chinchu is one of the made-up names for my son. He read the book and could appreciate it – a green signal for me.

You will read about an iPad transforming into something else. This is Ravi Kumar's idea. His eBook's idea: "Do Not Buy Gaming Consoles, Buy This Instead!" was born simultaneously. If this is a relevant interest for your child, I would recommend buying it. It can save you a lot of money over time instead of gaming consoles. The foundational principles of this book and Ravi's book are similar.

Ashal Jauhari, whose generosity allows me to function in the Facebook group, Asan Ideas for Wealth (AIFW). The members of the group who helped me set the tone of the book. I thank Harshini for readily agreeing to illustrate the book. Do follow her work via Instagram @harshini_arts

I thank all the reviewers, Jothi Padmanabhan, Rajkumar, Ananth, Upasana Mondal and V Muthu Krishnan. Their feedback helped me fine-tune the text, firm up the logic and eliminate embarrassing errors.

The encouragement from freefincal and AIFW communities is immense. Without this, I would have never got this idea; I would have never got the courage to write this.

Sincerely yours,
Pattu
Jan 13th, 2021

Prologue

Dear parent, let us take a moment and define this book's context; why I wrote it and what you can expect from it. This is not a book about investing, about beating inflation, etc. I have written this for children between the ages of 10 and 15.

So, there is little benefit in talking about inflation and equity investing to them. This is the age to lay the foundation for financial prudence. I asked myself, "if there is one thing, I would like to teach my child (who is almost 11 as I write this) about money management, what would it be?"

If my son understands the value of "think before you buy," if he understands the importance of understanding his needs, researching options available that would suit his needs, I will be happy.

Researching for options is the best way to delay gratification, avoid peer pressure and develop a sense of individuality (I will get what I want or need and not what others are buying). Other aspects covered are: 'we should differentiate between needs and wants'; 'we should not use debt for wants'; 'our needs include immediate needs and future needs'.

I would do my best to reiterate these four ideas to my son. The book stems from this goal. Concepts like inflation, saving vs investing can wait until 15-18. We cannot lecture or preach to children about these ideas. So, the text weaves around their typical desires often from what they see their friends' buy.

Each child is unique; each parent is different. The choices represented in the book are typical. However, they may or may not reflect your child's preferences. Therefore, you must read the book before presenting it to your child.

If you feel the items mentioned in the book do not reflect your child's tastes or the values you would like to instil in them, you can simply apply the template discussed in the book to their wants without showing them the book.

You can use this book in different ways. (1) Read it and talk to your child about it. (2) Read it with your child providing explanations along the way; (3) Ask your child to read and encourage her to ask questions. Naturally, you are the best to judge its usage.

Please read this in full before exposing it to the child. If I may suggest, encourage the child to discuss her thoughts with you as they read through. Personal finance is a vast topic. There will always be ideas that are too complex for some children; some issues you consider essential left out, and so on. You can let me know what you think about the book via email: freefincal@gmail.com

Disclaimer: All gadgets and devices mentioned in the book are only for illustrative purposes and are not recommendations. Kindly use your superpower to determine suitability :)

Pattu

Jan 12th 2021

To The Young Reader

You should have realised by now, looking at adults around you, that money plays a vital role in our daily lives. In this book, we meet Chinchu and her parents and learn about decision-making and money management related to two of her birthday-wishes.

I hope it would be interesting for you to learn how Chinchu got what she wanted for her birthday and in the process develops a superpower! You can guess what it is before I reveal it and discuss it with your parents!

I hope you will apply the book's ideas the next time you want your parents to buy you something. Tell your parents what you think about the book. They will convey it.

I look forward to your message. I wish you the best.

Pattu

CHAPTER ONE

CHINCHU WANTS AN IPAD FOR HER BIRTHDAY!

Chinchu had just finished dinner and sat to watch YouTube on Amma's laptop: 8:30 to 9:30 p.m. was her computer time - when she did not have tests, that is. Before she could start her first video, Appa wanted her to come to the hall for a few minutes.

"Why?" she asked. "Just for a few minutes, come on," Appa held out his hand.

Appa sat next to Amma and asked, "What do you want for your 10th birthday?"

Chinchu took a moment to think, hesitated, and replied, "iPad Air."

Chinchu noticed her parents' eyes open wide. They looked at each other, and seemed like they had made a mistake in asking her.

Amma was the first to recover, "Why do you need it?"

"Two of my classmates already have one, and it would be nice if I have one too."

"Hmm, I meant, what do you wish to do with it?" asked Amma.

"Watch my classes and use it for homework."

"Is that all you wish to do with it?" asked Amma, shifting her eyebrows.

"Er yes and anything else that we can do with it," said Chinchu, unsure of her answer.

"Right!" joined in Appa, "our baby is becoming a big girl! It is time for some research. We would like you to discover the following."

He took a piece of paper and wrote:

1. What will you do with the iPad?
2. What is the cost of the iPad? How much money should we spend to get it?

He showed the paper to Chinchu and asked, "how long would it take for you to find answers to these?"

"Tomorrow?" said Chinchu.

"Good. After dinner then."

The next day, Chinchu asked Amma, "how do I find the cost of the iPad, Amma?"

Amma opened a new tab in the browser, clicked the mike symbol and spoke: "what is the cost of iPad Air?"

She then clicked on the Apple website link, clicked the blue "buy" button on the top right, and scrolled down. She took a moment to read and said, "about 55 to 60 thousand rupees." The number seemed to trouble her.

"Will you get it for me, Amma?" asked Chinchu.

"Let us discuss tonight and then decide. Have you answered the first question?" asked Amma.

"Yes, I will show you tonight," said Chinchu.

After dinner, Appa asked Chinchu if she was ready.

"Yes, Amma told me that the iPad costs 55 to 60 thousand rupees, and these are things I want to do with it," Chinchu showed them a list.

1. Watch classes.
2. Do homework.
3. Watch YouTube.
4. Play Games.

Appa read it and said, "okay, do you know what our - Amma's and Appa's monthly income is? Do you know how much money we get for the work we do?"

"No"

"Rs. 50,000. Now what you are asking is more than that. Do not worry, we will not say no, but I have a suggestion to make, and if we buy this, it will come with some conditions. Are you okay with that?"

This worried Chinchu but saying no would mean no iPad, so she said, "yes" not sure what the suggestion and conditions were.

Amma now said, "We would like to buy something even better than an iPad for you, something that will help you with your needs today and tomorrow. Are you game?"

"Yes," said Chinchu, more curious than enthusiastic.

"If you are patient and pay attention to what we are doing, you will get a nice, sleek, fast desktop computer; but since the cost is too high for our income, we will buy it piece by piece over the next seven months."

"A desktop?" asked Chinchu, disappointed.

"Don't worry, it will be fast, and you will get a nice big screen with it. It will be a lot more comfortable than that iPad, and you can do a lot more with it."

"Er okay, but why seven months?"

"That is the time it would approximately take to get the parts of the computer; We can buy it all at once, but it is too expensive for our income."

"But," said Chinchu, still disappointed.

"After seven months, will you not be using the computer?' Will you not need it for classes and YouTube?" asked Amma.

'Yes, I am disappointed that I have to wait that long."

"We can only buy what we can and when we can buy it according to our income, Chinchu. Life is all about adjusting and adapting. This is your first life lesson!"

"Okay, thank you," said Chinchu, not convinced, but ready to leave the "meeting."

"Hang on, said Amma. You have accepted our suggestion. Now hear our conditions."

"Uh oh," thought Chinchu.

1. Taking care of the computer is your responsibility. I will show you how, but you must clean it at least once a week.
2. Your marks should increase from now since you have help. If they decrease, we will restrict the time you spend with it.
3. Whether it is schoolwork or fun, you will use your computer only during set hours. Just like you have your YouTube time after dinner. Nothing changes. If you violate this, "you will restrict the time you spend with it "completed Chinchu.
4. If you wish to do something new with the machine, you will ask our permission and proceed **if** we say "yes."
5. You will pay close attention to each item's price we will buy for this computer and once a month you will sit with us for a "money lesson."

"Are you okay with all these?"

"Yes, Amma," said Chinchu, wondering if she should have asked something else now.

"What is a money lesson?"

"Don't worry, it will be fun," said Appa.

The next day, Appa called a 'meeting" again. "What now?" thought Chinchu.

"We will buy this computer over the next seven months. We are in February now, so March, April, May, June, July, August, September. By the first or second week of September, we can buy the computer."

"From February, we will take Rs. 5,000 from our income and save it for buying the computer. Can you tell me the total cost of the computer?"

"So, 5000 x 7. Seven fives are 35, so 5000 x 7 = Rs 35,000."

Enter Caption

"Good. We will save this money and buy computer parts from time to time. Why don't you watch a few videos about the parts of a desktop computer on YouTube so you can understand what is happening?" suggested Appa.

"Are you buying this computer instead of the iPad because we do not have money to buy it immediately? Because you can buy the computer in pieces and not the iPad?" asked Chinchu.

Amma said, "We are buying the desktop because it is much better for you than the iPad. Yes, we are buying the computer in pieces because we cannot afford to buy it immediately."

"Most people have only limited money to work with, and we must do the best with what we can," said Amma.

"Okay, Amma," said Chinchu, still not convinced but had enough of this money talk.

CHAPTER TWO

CHINCHU RANKS THE FAMILY EXPENSES

Next month, it was time for Chinchu's first money lesson. "Tell me things we buy every month," said Amma.

"milk, vegetables, biscuits?"

Yes, we also pay for petrol to move around, we buy water cans, we buy internet/broadband so we can watch videos or do work, pay for mobile bills, purchase rice, dal, the cereal you eat, chocolates, chips, namkeen (salted snack items), pizza and so on."

"Now, what is our monthly income?"

"50,000 rupees?" answered Chinchu.

"Right, you remembered! Do you know what the word *prioritise* means?"

"No"

"Suppose our income gets reduced by half, say, Rs. 25,000, what items will you buy first?"

Chinchu thought for a few seconds and said, "food and internet?"

"Yes, we need food to survive, but not all food items are *essential*. For example, we can survive without snacks or pizza but need to buy vegetables, rice and dal."

"Similarly, we need to buy petrol to go to the office or go out. Whether they hold your classes online or at school, we need the internet. Same goes for us. Whether Appa and Amma work from home or go to the office, we need the internet."

"However, if we have less money to spend, we may not buy petrol more often and walk or hire an auto when we can. Similarly, we may reduce our internet speed and choose a less expensive plan."

"Deciding what expenses are more important; deciding what expenses are unnecessary and deciding what expenses are necessary, but what we can reduce is something we do every month even if our income did not decrease. Let us call this ranking or grading expenses, just like in school.

It is ranking them from most-important to less-important to non-important. This is **prioritising**," explained Amma.

"Now, if our income reduced to Rs. 25,000, would we still be able to spare Rs. 5000 a month to buy a computer?"

"I guess no ?" said Chinchu.

"Why?"

"Because we may then not have enough money to pay for food, petrol, internet."

"Excellent. See, you just prioritised. You ranked expenses or decided that certain expenses were more important than others. We can also look at it another way: if we first allocate our money to essential expenses, we will not have enough to spare for the less important ones."

"Food, petrol, internet or anything that we cannot live without or anything that would affect our daily life are called **needs**."

"Toys, ordering pizza, eating out, buying snacks, going to the movies, watching movies online, watching YouTube," Amma paused looking into Chinchu's eyes to see if she understood, "are not essential. We can live without these. We call these **wants**."

"Needs = now; Wants = wait; is a way for you to remember this."

Enter Caption

"Next year, we would need to pay your school tuition fees; When you finish school, we need to pay college fees; These are **future needs**. We are setting aside money each month for these needs from our income."

"Fortunately, our income has not reduced and is still Rs. 50,000. However, if we consider all our present needs and plan for our future needs, add some of our wants like snacks and eating out, we may still be Rs. 1000 short of the Rs. 5000 needed for your computer. So, what do we do?"

"Cut down the snacks and eat out less?" said Chinchu.

"Good. Are you ready to sacrifice this for seven months so we can get the missing Rs 1000 each month? This only means fewer snacks than usual. Are you okay with this?"

"Yes, Amma"

"Good. Tomorrow let us plan this out."

CHAPTER THREE

CHINCHU USES THE ENVELOPE SYSTEM

The next day, Amma and Appa called Chinchu into the bedroom. She saw several boxes and envelopes (covers) all over the bed.

Appa noticed Chinchu's puzzled, almost scared look, and said, "remember what Amma taught about needs and wants yesterday?"

"yes, need-now, wants-wait," said Chinchu, looking for Amma's approval and got it quicker than she expected.

Appa continued, "Good, now we would like you to see this in action. Each month after we get our salary, we sit down and put it in these boxes and covers or envelopes. Would you like to participate this month?"

Enter Caption

“Yes.” said Chinchu, thinking, “What choice do I have? If I say no, I say no to the computer too!”

Appa asked Chinchu to enter the amounts he says in his computer. “If you wish to know what the money is for, ask,” said Amma.

“Emergency fund Rs. 1000” Appa said and put that amount in a box labelled “for emergencies only.”

Then he said “Milk: Rs. 2500” and put that amount in a cover labelled ‘Milk’.

Before he could say the next item, Amma stopped him and asked Chinchu, “do you know what the emergency fund is for?”

“No.”

“If our computers or TV or washing machine breaks down, we will need extra money to repair. We cannot take it from our salary. We need it for normal expenses. We have created an emergency stash of cash, which we use if there are sudden expenses we did not plan. Makes sense?" asked Amma. Chinchu nodded.

Chinchu then entered amounts for water, flat maintenance charges, vegetables, groceries, petrol, broadband, and so on.

It went on and on that Chinchu wondered if any money would remain for the computer. She was waiting for that Rs. 5000 Amma and Appa said they would allocate for the computer.

Appa said to Amma, "We will take Rs. 2000 from the college fund, Rs. 2000 from retirement and set it for the computer." Now he turned to Chinchu and said, the remaining Rs. 1000 we will take from *snacks and eating out* as we agreed earlier. We then must spend less on these. Is that understood?"

Chinchu nodded but felt a little uneasy while hearing this. Amma sensed it and explained.

"Each month we set aside money for retirement. That is for a time when we will be too old to work and will not get a salary."

"We also set aside money for your college education. Each year we need to pay school fees. So, we take money from our salary and keep it someplace safe like the bank."

"Since we need to find Rs. 5000 for your computer for the next seven months, we must reduce the money we set aside for future needs and allocate it for the computer."

"Can we take more from the eating out cover Amma, as this is a **want**?"

"Thank you, but we already have reduced this spending by more than half. We need to find a balance between our needs and wants. We will manage, but I am glad you asked."

said Amma.

"Is it going to be difficult for you to find this money for the computer?" asked Chinchu, worried for the first time more about what her parents had to do rather than about something she wanted.

Appa looked at Amma for a moment and said, "Well ... getting this computer will mean two things for seven months: (1) we must spend less on snacks and eating out and (2) set aside lesser money for future needs, but we will manage. We are glad it worries you, but you have been a good girl, and we think you deserve it."

"Thank you, Appa, but ..."

"Yes, what is it?"

"Maybe you can get me a less expensive computer?" asked Chinchu.

"We discussed that," said Amma, "I think considering your future use, we could buy a better model and use it for a few years. We can also upgrade it in future."

"Don't worry; we will manage. We want you to see us put different expenses in different covers to understand how we manage our money each month. We call this the **envelope system**."

"This month we have reduced the spending on snacks and eating out from Rs. 1500 to Rs. 500. This means, no matter what, we should not spend more than Rs. 500 this month on snacks and ordering out. The envelope system allows you to set aside money for different expenses and set a limit which we have to obey."

"We call this a budget. We divide our income into three sections: (1) present needs, (2) present wants and (3) future needs and wants."

"Okay, things like food and the internet are present needs, eating out is a present want and my school fee, college fee and the computer are future needs and wants. Am I right?" asked Chinchu.

"Perfect. We have budgeted for this month!" said Appa as they put all covers and boxes back into shelves.

CHAPTER FOUR

USING A CREDIT CARD

Though Chinchu's parents wanted her to study about money only once a month, she slowly saw its role everywhere. When she sat down for the budgeting the next month, she noticed an entry in Appa's budget sheet called charity and Rs. 2000 marked against it and asked what it was.

Appa said, "there are many families less fortunate than us, and many parents do not have money even for basic needs. We are helping a family pay a child's school fee under a plan a KEY: Kid's Education and You[1]."

Chinchu wondered why some children could get anything they want, and some children could not get even some things they needed.

"That is a deep question!" smiled Amma, "We will talk about that soon."[2]

Another entry was income tax. "What is this?" Chinchu asked.

"It is money we give to the government from our income to help it build roads, put up streetlights, pay people who clean our roads, pay our police officers and so on."

"Just like our salary is an income, tax is one form of income for the government to run our country. You will learn more about this when you earn money," Appa explained, and Chinchu nodded.

Soon Appa bought the components for her computer. Since she had by now watched several videos on this, she knew what each part was.

Each time they delivered an item, she noted its name and searched on YouTube for more information about it. She now knew what kind of motherboard her computer would have, what kind of processor, hard disk, and the RAM.

As she saw each video, she seemed to become more and more impressed with what she was getting instead of the iPad. She was now looking forward to using the assembled computer.

One day, she accompanied Amma to the supermarket. For the first time, she was turning every packet in every direction to find out its price. At the counter, she saw Amma use a card instead of cash for the items. So, she later asked. "How does this work Amma?"

[1] Learn more about KEY here: **Melvin Joseph's KEY**

[2] Talking to My Daughter About the Economy by Yanis Varoufakis is a good book for this.

Enter Caption

Amma thought for a moment and said, “Good question, let us discuss this after dinner.”

That night, the family gathered, and Amma began, “I used a **credit card** in the store today. We purchased items for Rs. 2000, and I borrowed this money from the company who gave us this card with the condition I pay them once a month.”

For example, “if I spend Rs. 1000 on the 2nd of the month, spend Rs. 1500 on the 12th and spend Rs. 1000 on the 20th, I must pay the total amount spent: 1000 + 1500 + 1000 = Rs. 3500 by the 28th.”

“I have temporarily borrowed money (electronically) from the card company and paid the shopkeeper. The card company will earn a small fee from this sale. Are you with me so far?" asked Amma, Chinchu nodded. Amma now took a paper where she had made a table and read from it.

"If I do not pay this Rs. 3500 by the 28th, I pay a fine every day. The fine will keep increasing every day so fast that if I do not pay this amount for one month, I must pay an extra Rs. 106 (3500 + 106)."

"If I delay the payment by two months, I have to pay Rs. 216; three months delay the fine increases to Rs. 329 and so on."

"If I do not pay for one year, the fine will grow to Rs. 1541. I spent only Rs. 3500 but because I could not pay it to the card company, I had to pay a fine that rapidly increases each day. I do not expect you to understand how it increases. It is enough if you understand the fine increases quickly, okay?" asked Amma.

"Okay"

"Now, tell me what we should do to ensure we do not waste money on these fines?" asked Appa.

"Pay before the due date?" answered Chinchu.

"Correct! Pay the entire amount you spent before the due date. Now, we could have used the credit card and paid for the computer immediately, and you could use it now. Why did we not?"

Chinchu had a blank expression on her face. She felt sorry she did not know the answer.

"Hey, this is not something you should remember! Take this pen and paper, calculate and tell us," said Appa.

Chinchu took it but did not know what to do. So Amma asked, "how much money are we keeping aside every month for the computer?"

"Rs. 5000."

"Good, how long should we save this?"

"Seven months."

"So, what is the cost of the computer?"

"Oh, 35,000 rupees sorry!"

"No need to be sorry; there is no need to remember it! You could have asked for our monthly budget sheet and looked it up that we have allocated Rs. 5000 for seven months."

"This is not a quote from-memory question! Work out the answer with the data available. No need to remember anything. Okay?" Chinchu nodded.

"So, the cost of the computer is Rs. 35,000, and we could simply go to the store, give the shopkeeper our card, for making the sale and get the computer home."

"Why didn't we?"

There was silence for a few seconds as Chinchu's eyes moved left and right as she thought hard. Appa was about to say something, but Amma stopped him by placing her hand on him.

"Oh, right! Your income is Rs. 50,000 and if you borrow Rs. 35,000 from the card, pay it back by the 28th, or you must pay a fine. You cannot pay that much because we have other expenses."

Amma and Appa both said "precisely" looked at each other and smiled with satisfaction.

"Can I ask one more question?" asked Amma. Chinchu nodded.

"Suppose we use the card for Rs. 35,000, get you the computer and pay the card company Rs. 5000 each month but the catch is we have to pay this for eight months, do you think it is a good idea?"

"I suppose no because we will then spend Rs. 5000 more?" said Chinchu, not sure if that is the full answer.

"That is correct. You know how we save that Rs. 5000 every month - by putting away less for our future needs:

retirement and your college education fund. Remember?" said Amma, Chinchu nodded.

"The cost of the computer is Rs. 35,000, but the cost of having it immediately is Rs. 35,000 + Rs.5000. You do not need the computer immediately. Our retirement and your college education fund are more important. So, we chose not to use the card for this expense."

"When Amma used the card in the supermarket today, it was for our regular expenses. We could have paid cash for it, but I chose the card. This way, I need not carry too cash much when I go out. Makes sense?"

"Yes," said Chinchu.

"The moral of the story is, use the credit card only as a replacement of cash *you already have*. Never use it to buy anything that you do not need in a hurry, that you can purchase later with cash."

"One last question: We keep aside Rs 5000 every month for seven months. Can I then use the credit card for buying the computer?" asked Appa.

Chinchu thought for a few seconds and said, "Yes, we can because we already have the Rs. 35,000 and can pay the money back to the card company in time."

"Fantastic. That is enough money talk, off you go."

CHAPTER FIVE

THE COMPUTER ARRIVES!

The day that Chinchu was waiting for seven months finally arrived. Appa brought the computer and set it up. Chinchu learnt how to use the computer over the next few weeks.

Almost a month later, Appa asked, “do you know why we got you the computer rather than the iPad?”

“Because I could do more with it, and you can buy it in pieces?” asked Chinchu.

“Hmm, not just that. Every year they will release a new iPad model. Those who have iPads in your class must buy the new model if they want to upgrade. In your case, we can always upgrade any part individually and make the machine faster for the next seven years at least if you maintain it properly.”

Chinchu now realised that what she got was better than what she wanted only when her friends came to see the new “machine.” Their expressions of “wow” and “cool” made her feel smart and satisfied.

Enter Caption

After the initial excitement about the computer toned down, the family sat down for another meeting after dinner.

"Chinchu, what have you learnt from this computer-buying episode?" asked Amma.

Chinchu thought and said, "We must look at our income and needs before buying something?"

"Good. That is true. If we wish to buy something, we must," Amma took a pen and pad and wrote.

"First and most important: never wish for something just because your friends got it, or relatives got it. You have your own needs and wants. Buy stuff that satisfies these conditions after these checks."

"Second: Understand our requirement. For example, you wanted an iPad initially. What you wanted was a computing machine to do your work. So, write what tasks you want it for."

"Third: Make a list of all the items that satisfy your requirements. For example, you can work on a desktop more comfortably than with an iPad. You type more comfortably, use a mouse happily, etc. So, you choose items that will work for you and reject items that will not. Does that make sense?"

Chinchu now appreciated why her parents got the desktop instead of the iPad. It was not just the cost. It was about her requirements!

"Fourth: Which device can we change easily if your needs increase in future? For example, if tomorrow you wish to run a program for your school project requiring more RAM, we can simply buy that alone instead of buying a whole new machine. Got it?"

"Fifth: Now, you have a list of devices that will suit your requirement and that you will not have to change often. You now look at the price and ask which of these can I afford?"

"Sixth: Ask, do I need it immediately, or could I wait while I save up enough money to buy it? For example, today, a computer is a 'need', but it is not an 'urgent need'. You could wait for it. Yes?" Chinchu nodded again.

"Seventh Now, you are ready to either buy or plan the purchase. You must look at your income, look at your expenses, and note down how you will accommodate this purchase or the monthly saving required. Remember what we did the first time you saw us with the covers and boxes?"

"The moral of the story is, we must not be in a hurry to buy stuff without understanding what we want/need, researching for products that satisfy our requirements and planning how we will buy it," said Amma and gave the pad with the list to Chinchu.

"The next time you want something for your birthday. Follow the points in this list!" Seeing Chinchu's worried face, Amma added, "don't worry, we will help."

CHAPTER SIX

TELESCOPE VS BINOCULARS!

Over the next few months, it thrilled Chinchu to use her new computer - each time Amma and Appa let her operate it, that is. Soon the months rolled on and her 11th birthday was round the corner.

Appa called Chinchu to the hall one day. “Your next birthday is coming soon, but we cannot get you anything expensive this time. As you know, the computer cost us more money. We will get you something nice and small this time, but think of something bigger for your next birthday, but it has to be something you need to use outside, not inside the house!”

Chinchu understood. She was not disappointed because she knew Amma and Appa had to do to buy the computer.

Chinchu had a keen interest in astronomy. Amma had given Chinchu all her old books about planets and galaxies earlier. She could learn more about them with her computer and realised there were many recent developments.

So, it was easy to find an “outdoors gift”. She wanted a telescope.

She proudly announced it to Amma and Appa. She expected them to be proud of her choice - this was not a "gadget," it was a piece of scientific equipment.

Amma and Appa exchanged glances, and Amma said, "Do you know what it means to use a telescope?"

Chinchu did not follow the question, so she said "no" hoping Amma would explain.

Amma took out a pad and pen again, and Chinchu thought to herself, "uh oh."

"Find out which is better for you, a telescope or binoculars. To do this, you must be clear about what you want to see: just the moon and the planets or star clusters and nebulae? All this I am hoping will come out from your research - use your computer wisely!"

"However, there are things you must understand. This may not be as expensive as your computer, but it would be a waste of money if you do not use it regularly."

"Using it means going to the terrace, waiting for 15-20 minutes in the dark to get your eyes adjusted and then patiently scanning the sky. This will take time, at least another 30-60 minutes."

"Face mosquito bites sacrifice your computer time, and **regularly** use the device - at least once a week. If you are not willing to do this, it would be a waste of money."

"We will not appreciate it if, after buying, you lose interest after a few months. It is unlikely you would lose interest in using your computer, but this - very possible because it takes effort to set it up and patience to view the sky."

"If it rains, you cannot use it, if it is cloudy, you cannot use it and worse from our house, what you can watch could be limited because of the light from surrounding buildings (light pollution). So do not expect to see everything bright and clear as they show in photos from NASA or in astronomy books or videos."

"Now we want you to think about this for a week and come back to us with your decision."

Chinchu nodded and learned more about telescopes and binoculars. The differences between the two, what kind of telescope or binocular to buy, and so on. As she did this, the desire to go out and watch the sky increased.

A week later, Amma asked, "are you ready to let us know if you have the discipline to use the telescope or would you like something else?"

Chinchu said she was ready. Amma continued, "if you lose interest or if you forget to go upstairs at least once a week because you were busy with your new computer, all your gifts for the next three years will be less than Rs. 500. Is that understood?"

"Yes, Amma, I am ready," Chinchu ran back to her room and got a pad. "I have to learn more about telescopes and binoculars."

It delighted Amma to hear this. "Excellent, and what does your research show?"

"I learnt that it would be hard to look at the sky for long via telescopes. Binoculars would be easier for a beginner to use."

"Any magnification about 10X is hard to hold in hand (because we have a natural shake) that is why all telescopes which have higher magnification than binos always come with a tripod."

"Binoculars have a larger field of view, but you cannot zoom in too much to see details. Telescopes have a smaller field of view, but you zoom in closer to see details like Saturn's rings."

Appa hugged Chinchu in admiration so tightly when he heard this that Chinchu thought she would choke!

"Fantastic! It delights us you have used the computer well," said Amma, "so now you must decide what you want: the convenience of binos or the precision of a telescope. Do you need to see the rings of Saturn or the clouds of Jupiter or do you want to see star clusters?"

Chinchu wanted to say "both," but resisted. Amma continued, "Each one has a different use, but let us start with a binocular. You can get used to stargazing with this and maybe after a couple of years we shall think of a good telescope IF you use this regularly and are still interested."

"Now we have decided what to buy, take a week, compare bino models and make a list," said Appa.

So Chinchu learned more about binoculars. She watched several videos of astronomers reviewing binoculars.

It was time to present the results. So, she made a PowerPoint presentation. "We use two numbers to specify binos: For example, 10 x 50. Here 10 refers to the magnification and 50 mm is the diameter of the objective (the front lens)."

"Larger the objective, the better, as they can collect more light. Larger the magnification the better, but any magnification above 10X would need a tripod as it would be heavy."

"The binoculars suitable for astronomy are:

10X magnification with 50 mm objective,

12 X magnification with 60 mm objective

etc. going up to

25X magnification with 100 mm objective."

"Have you been paying attention to the price?" asked Appa.

"Yes Appa, the 10 x 50 is about Rs. 5000-6000, the 12 x 60 Rs. 9000-10,000 and so on."

Appa looked at Amma. "If we were living in the outskirts of the city with few lights, we could get away with a 10 x50, and this does not need a tripod," said Amma.

"For our neighbourhood, 12x 60 is the minimum I would try, and this needs a tripod as it would weigh about a kilogram."

"And the tripod?" asked Appa. "It would be at least Rs. 5000- 7000 with a three-way pan head that can handle about two kilos of weight," said Amma.

"Chinchu, have you been looking at telescope prices too?" asked Appa.

"Yes, Appa, the reviews I saw mention that a good one would cost about Rs. 35,000"

Amma thought and said, "Okay Chinchu, like with the computer (and anything else in life) we must find a balance between what we want and what we can afford and what is available."

"We can afford the 12x60 + tripod for about Rs. 15,000-16,000, and you can use it for basic astronomy. You cannot expect significant results with it but show us you are interested enough to go to the terrace and use it regularly; we will consider a good telescope after a couple of years."

"We can also use the 12x60 binos during the day, for example, bird watching. It will not be a waste of money if you lose interest in astronomy later (which is not a crime!). Does this make sense?"

Chinchu nodded.

"Okay, in the next few days, list the companies that manufacture 12x60 binos and suitable tripods. Next month when we sit for our budget, we shall allocate money for this."

"Chinchu, we are very proud of the way you did your research, studying options, understanding what you can do with each, what is suitable for you and what we can afford."

"Remember to do this for everything you purchase when you earn money on your own. Also, remind us to do this if we forget!"

Chinchu with her new binoculars!

CHAPTER SEVEN

CHINCHU'S SUPERPOWER

Dear reader, if you have reached this point by reading the previous chapters one after another, I thank you for your attention. We are now at the end of a small thread in Chinchu's life.

For a book titled "Chinchu Gets a Superpower!" you may have wondered why you did not read about any such power so far. I revealed the superpower in the first chapter when Chinchu wanted an iPad.

We shall discuss this on the next page, but before you scroll down, can you take a moment to think about it and tell your parents what it is? I am sure it would delight them to know your thoughts on this.

↓

↓

↓

↓

↓

↓

↓

↓

Let us go back to the events of Chapter 1. Chinchu wanted an iPad only because her friends got it. If the family purchased the iPad, they would have to limit their actions by what the device can do. Next year, there will be a new iPad model, and Chinchu would feel like she is using an old gadget and would want to "upgrade."

Instead, Chinchu (and her parents) focused on her requirements: What does she want and what device would suit her requirements for the money they can spend?

Put your requirements first and purchases last. If we reverse these steps, it would be like putting the cart before the horse!

Enter Caption

The superpower Chinchu got from her parents is this ability to understand her requirements first. That is why she could appreciate the differences between a telescope and a binocular and understand what would suit her better.

It is a superpower because, with so many products to choose from, it is impossible to choose unless we know what we want. If we know what we want precisely, choosing becomes simpler and easier.

Between the first step (understanding requirements), and the last step (purchasing the product), comes the product research and planning.

Product research: Chinchu's parents found the computer configuration suitable for her needs, and Chinchu herself studied the different telescopes and binoculars available.

Planning: Chinchu's parents adjusted their monthly budget, allocated Rs. 5000 a month and planned to buy the computer in seven months.

As you grow older, you will encounter new products; you will have additional needs and wants.

If you apply this superpower before you make a purchase, you can buy confidently. If you liked this idea and use it, let me know how it went :)

It is time for me to say goodbye now. Please discuss these ideas with your parents. I will be happy to hear what you thought about this book. Write me a note! I wish you all the best for your future.

> "*"To be yourself in a world constantly trying to make you something else is the greatest accomplishment."*
>
> *Ralph Waldo Emerson*"

Enter Caption

www.ingramcontent.com/pod-product-compliance
Lightning Source LLC
LaVergne TN
LVHW021145160826
845679LV00023B/2060

* 9 7 9 8 8 9 1 3 3 5 5 2 3 *